# Two Legends

John Watson

# Two Legends

*Two Legends*
ISBN 978 1 76041 964 6
Copyright © John Watson 2020

First published 2020 by
**Ginninderra Press**
PO Box 3461 Port Adelaide 5015
www.ginninderrapress.com.au

# Contents

| | |
|---|---|
| Frank O'Hara Poems | 7 |
| Interlude | 67 |
| Cupid and Psyche | 73 |

# Frank O'Hara Poems

It is one of the more pleasing commonplaces of twentieth century poetry that Frank O'Hara regularly spent his lunch hour from the Metropolitan Museum of Art composing poems at demonstration typewriters in various locations. This notion is the subject of the variations that follow.

# Obituary

Frank O'Hara (1926–1966)

One minute (filled
Amusingly with crowds,
Greetings, smiles, bells,
Edifices of traffic,
Sirens, birds, oceans)
He was typing
Poems at lunch
On demonstration machines
In typewriter shops;
The next, suddenly,
A reversing vehicle
On Fire Island
Had despatched him
To that flux
In the sky
Where any number
Of simultaneous collisions
Of oceans, bells,
Traffic of edifices,
Sirens, smiles, greetings,
Could be written
Simply by virtue
Of being there,
Like a thousand
Everests floating by,
Each eminently available,
A continuous, delicious,
Endless, strolling lunch.

# Tomorrow is Another Day

On his way to Bloomingdales
Through a sneak preview of weather
Including the sun saying, 'Meet me after work
But I'm not promising anything, mind,'
Or clouds unrolling some pleasant new alphabet,

He is determined this time to succeed,
As he did not quite yesterday,
To seize rhetoric and wring its neck.
And he strides with apparent nonchalance
To the typewriters on display.

# A Visit to the Library

One lunch hour as the clock announces the present
Taking off in its mad rush into the past
He hares into not the typewriter shop but the library.

Outside amongst the plane-trees, leaving aside
The surrogate multiplicity of the library,
He notes the smell of nail polish remover

While an automatic tendency towards apposition
Is readily corrected by looking out from the window
And seeing there things indifferent and independent:

Children, for example, with helium-filled balloons,
Or the deconstruction of the concert ramparts scaffolding,
Or the service vehicle nudging the lemon-scented gums.

Inside, in the leafy grove of the library
The smell of camphor laurel drifts among the stacks
Legitimising a general desire for effusion.

When, after a minor fire alarm, the windows are opened,
The open windows suggest a rain of stolen books
Thrown down to accomplices amongst the trees.

And just when you thought it was safe to reach out
For a definitive statement or two, a truckload of new
Acquisitions reverses through the kapok trees.

# Parallel Universes

Meanwhile lunch went on pangrammatically
With his variations on *the quick brown fox*,
And occasionally his *box with five dozen
Liquor jugs* and conceits involving someone
Taking to task the lazy dog –
These from scraps of paper left
In the typewriter carriage with traces of lettuce.

At this very same hour of salad on rye
Unknown to our skywriting typist
Someone else was composing elsewhere,
One day an arabesque, another day an impromptu,
Another an alternative to the dominant-tonic
Dominance of the eight-bar blues,
On a keyboard in a Steinway showroom.

And in a glass-walled department store
Approximately equidistant from these two
Someone else was composing shadows
And framing suggestive likenesses
In a Polaroid demonstration booth
Separated from the real world by a revolving door
(While outside a lazy dog wagged its tail).

# Grandstand Tetralogues

The day invites elaboration.
Fountain pen sculptors repair
To the velodrome cafeteria.
Seated at a table
Where snapdragons are luridly
Brushed with dry pigment,
They discuss suitable openings
For a poem. 'Yippee'
Is Frank's suggestion. Hasn't
Ken already used it?
'I don't think so,'
Says Frank with increasing
Conviction. 'I'm sure now.
"Hooray" and "Ugh" and
Possibly "Doggone" and "Wow"
But definitely not "Yippee".'
The cyclists whizz by.
The lissom waitress brings
Orchidaceous glazed cereal bowls
And adjusts the snapdragons.
Dawn accompanies our breakfast.
Snap Crackle and Pop
Drown out further discussion.
The sky is ultramarine.
The marina is azure.
Views from the grandstand
Of skydivers targeting waves
In the tarpaulin ocean
Are just so beautiful
They agree to abandon

This conference on gelato
And leave at once
To work them in –
Every item on show –
As an opening line.

# Poem With the 6th, 7th and Last Lines Rhyming

In the museum library one notes with amusement
The way the catalogue print-out stops abruptly at
The end of every line with consequent truncation
Like Cinemascope movie titles on afternoon television; thus,
*Frank O'Hara a comprehensive bi*
*Meditations upon an emergency po*
*Larry Rivers I Remember Frank OH*
Also in the stairwell it is beguiling
(A word our dedicatee used frequently and resonantly)
To see a blank wall with a faint outline
Of dust where once a picture hung,
And in its place a trace of *sfumato* and below it
The title 'Untitled'.

And on the shelves
A plethora of books by and celebrating
Frank O'Hara tend to the very bottom shelf
Requiring one almost to lie down to peruse them
In which position several adolescent silk skirts
Step over and brush past the recumbent. And then remarkably,
As remarkable as white cockatoos suddenly leaving the magnolias
When a storm is about to lash the harbour,
These books all in turn open at the same poem,
The one beginning, 'It's my lunch hour, so I go…'

## *Musica Ficta*

Like the flamenco scale
Hovering on the subdominant,
Not venturing upon melody
But rather contemplating it,

The typewriter lays open
The poem as chronicle
Of the creative impulse
Which produces it. Further,

It makes an aesthetic
Of not minding that
Past greatness no longer
Visits us, and that

Consistently the general effect
Is of language translated
From a primal tongue
Into something more cool,

Into language much accustomed
To technologies, to transmission
Along cables of glass
By repeated laser separations.

And if by chance
Some echo or resonance
Of past linguistic glory
Should attach itself fleetingly,

This is called 'poetic'
But only insofar as
It is perfectly clear
That such an effect

Was not solely intended.
Thus the poem proceeds
By fluttering over scales
Decorated by *musica ficta*,

While pretending to be
Almost oblivious of it.
So the whole tone
Scale, for example, encountering

A scattering of semi-tones,
May clearly signal
The perils of multiplicity,
The roads not taken.

All of these considerations
Signal with cheerful smiles
From the typewriter legions
Lining up for lunch.

# Smoking Days

In the days when everyone smoked
And to express reverie was to raise
Bette Davis eyes while engaging the mouth
With its fragrant token cylinder of paper

And conversation had its frequent analogue
In the cigarette tapped, the cigarette proffered,
The cigarette jittering between the lips,
The cigarette as baton directing accompaniments,

He stepped out into the smoking, glowing street,
Pausing at noon and in no haste to proceed,
Where everyone seemed enchantingly engrossed
In the jigsaw puzzle of yesterday –

Apparently they were left with all the difficult
Sky pieces. He used a cigarette to indicate
And activate various facades, while narrowly avoiding
An open manhole into which the sun

Had clearly fallen, to judge from the intense
Levels of radiation everywhere. It seeped from fences,
It gathered to a focus in hibiscus flowers,
It streamed from granite arcades and foyers,

Setting off alarm systems, pullulating,
Ringing front doorbells before running away,
Perplexing cats on lawns in front gardens,
Stirring wind chimes despite the still air.

What a day! So romantically
Like several others in recent memory,
He was won over and resolved he must
Collect the complete set! He must!

His only regret was not to have kept
More carefully the many similar days
Spiralling calmly in the sunlit air,
Days now valuable and not to be offered again.

The only solution was to light another
Pristine cigarette and proceed
To the nearest typewriter on 42nd Street
And wrest back a few of those days.

# Jogging

A ploughed-field sky,
An apple thrown into the yard,
Atalanta out jogging,
Every indication that the day

Will be surprising,
Intractable and headstrong
But oh, how adorable.
Obvious and inexplicable

Events already in place,
The front door open
On a hibiscus hedge
Brimming with news, the Atlantic,

A sea-fret still rising
On the face of the water,
A barge hastily acknowledging
Aeroplanes already up and about.

He showers and shaves
And breakfasts on champagne
And asparagus. He shaves
A peach, is ready to leave,

Again today armed with nothing
More than an eye to the main
Lovely vicissitudes of chance
And *qwertyuiop*.

## Shampoo

Turning round in the shower,
Hair a turban of water,

Head a hedge, he does not hear
Those shy creatures, born

Of any kind of sensory lapse
Or concentration of thought,

Enter through the locked front door.
Nor do they threaten him

But rather they bathe the hall
And the outdoors studio,

Nestled amongst vagrant nasturtiums
Shadowed only by the clothes line,

With such a benign strangeness
That, as he stands in the yard

Towelling his hair and occasionally
Seeing glimpses of starlings and the sky,

He feels the possibility of a vast
20th century *Orlando Furioso*

Set largely in the infinite city
To which he travels by ferry,

A self-perpetuating epic
With virtually no possible ending:

Sufficient to sustain him, by changing
Without his knowledge, it will grow old

As he grows old, and, from time to time,
Flood him with enswathing presence.

It only remains to get through to lunch
And a resplendent typewriter.

# Demolition Site

One day the typewriter shop was gone.
(He'd absent-mindedly taken the wrong

Last turning.) Where it should have been,
A caterpillar tractor (blue)

Was working conscientiously
Behind a paling and bindweed fence.

The excavation left unmoved
Part of the building on a plinth.

What irrepressible delight,
A momentary plume of happiness,

At such a perplexing gap in Nature
Before he realised in fact

He'd absent-mindedly taken the right
Last turning when it should be left.

But even at this subsidence
(His feelings and the gaping cave)

The stroboscopic fence allowed
Fermata into which he might

Insert cadenzas still. And so,
Aglow, his thought was like a glass

Whose orange zest and ice confuse,
And over which is poured Cointreau.

# Spiralling

In the mythology of the 20th century
                           no icon more enduring
Than the cigarette,
                  not as narcotic
But, for brief decades of medical innocence,
When light was a substance in the *film noir*
                        which could be poured like vermouth
And which fumed and overflowed every vessel,
As a sign of concentrated being
                    or thought made manifest.

Then the cigarette,
                    inseparable from every protagonist
                    against Art Deco drapes or glass
Or a gliding convertible
                  under dappled trees,
Served to unite the protagonist and action;
Cocteau used the cigarette
                  to convey Tristan's presence
In *L'Eternel Retour* at that very point
                  where Beroul's manuscript begins.
And in that silver world
                  as a node in the visible,
It became, like a vase of flowers or a telephone,
An accompaniment to whatever transaction
                    was to be seen as central
                    while its fumes clearly betoken,
While spiralling, some aspect of the spiritual.

All of this, and more, he will endeavour
                to remember and leave behind
Like disappearing question marks of smoke
Once he reaches the Sam Spade slatted blinds
                of the typewriter at lunch.

# Poetics

There must be typewriter poetry which is not
Simply an oblique way of saying something
That a reviewer will better express in prose,
Something that already everyone knows
And which has a sort of authentic ring.
Rather it should be like a hot

Day when we are aware of everything,
When everything is in a pronounced state
Of strident imploration, when afternoon rain
Is already almost graspable at noon,
Billowing out, crowding, everything precipitate,
The air like a hammock seen from below, or a swing

Jutting into our lives. It must have gaps
Between ideas as between stanzas, a breached wall
Like firing synapses. It must have, too,
Great leaps, enjambements like a kangaroo
Travelling. It must be untranslateable
And lean against Possibly and Perhaps,

An annexe propped against a caravan
Like a pack of cards. Some imminence
Announces itself up and down the coast;
We are in the bank vault for some kind of tryst,
Then we hear the roar, we see a flying fence –
The world has been levelled in a hurricane.

# Group Photograph

Back Row, L to R: Elaine De Kooning,
Frank and Eleanor Perry, Fairfield Porter,
Angelo Torricini, Arthur Gold,
Jane Wilson, Kenward Elmslie, Frank O'Hara,
Katherine Porter, Unidentified Lady.
Second Row, L to R: Steven Rivers,
Larry Rivers, Miriam Shapiro,
Sylvia Mazell, Robert Fizdale, Joan Ward,
Frank O'Hara, Paul Brach, Nancy Ward.
Front Row, Seated and Kneeling: Joe Hazan,
Bill Berkner, Frank O'Hara, William De Kooning,
Alvin Novak, Herbert Machez, Ken Koch.

The Unidentified Lady
                Identifies herself:
'We had just got back
                From boating on the river.
We'd moored the boat outside
                The university
In which we'd gone to see
                A demonstration
In their laboratories
                Of superfluidity,
Where supercooled liquid nitrogen flowed
                Over the edge of a bowl.
I remember Frank was loud
                In his celebratory praise.
And later, on the river,
                We thought the same thought,
That we were super-cool,

                That we were frictionless,
And so vocal and aglow
                As to overflow the boat.

Ken wrote an ode beginning,
                "Red Indian friends afloat
In our kayak on the ice lawns…"
                Frank wrote an ode beginning,
"Molecules holding hands
                Let friendship oil the walls…"
And Bill wrote an ode beginning,
                "Don't rock the boat
And don't knock the rock…"
                And Frank wrote an ode beginning,
"Niagara of nitrogen!
                Flowing uphill like salmon…"'
The Unidentified Lady
                Changes cells even as she speaks:
'I was their inspiration
                On this occasion on the river.
Slipping out of my clothes
                I dived into the dark
And surfaced. It seemed at that moment
                All my molecules dispersed
And I rose like a river wraith.
                Afterwards we showered
And Frank made tall cold blintzes
                And we went on gossiping
And everyone recited their odes
                While I dried my hair.

We sat in rows for a photograph
I was to be the unidentified lady
And took up my position. Now you'll recall
How, in the mystic East, or India,
A yogi or a mystic learns the art
Of disappearing from a photograph.
But Frank, you will have noted, contrariwise,
Contrived to be at once convivial
In every row, musing with everyone.'

# Summer Nights

Through open windows past the curtains
    Past the curtains thrown back,
Thrown back as if someone were sleeping,
    Throwing back the covers,
There one sees in every room
    Lit by a table lamp
A sombre photograph, darkly framed
    Of someone who has not returned
From some distant war,
    Or a print of fields

With trees discreetly standing to one side.
    Further on, where frangipani fall,
One hears the fall
    Of piano music: a certain air
Absolutely, irreversibly resolving
    A suspended dissonance,
The suspension
    Hanging in the air still,
The air still coloured by its fumes
    Coloured like tea infusing in a glass.

Tomorrow is another day,
    And in another department store
Another assistant curiously resembling Rhett Butler
    Will obligingly remove the cover
From another typewriter.

## Unexpected Purchase

One sunspilling lunch in the Bronx
In an emporium stacked to the gunwales
With second-hand typewriters
He manages to release poems
Which are so remarkably free of metaphor, rhetoric
And indeed all the devices of the Western tradition,
That in a daze he finds himself
Outside having purchased the machine
And having to carry it all the way
Back to the Museum of Modern Art.

# Swimming Pool

First and foremost, it is indolent:
It distances itself from any running rhythm,
Almost as if the sequence into which
Events are placed, like microchip components
On a conveyor belt,
    had been drawn out
So that a pause
Masks each unit of activity
Which could reasonably be called an event
Even though most of these 'events'
Lie just below the threshhold of potentiality
Like submarine life a few centimetres
    below the surface of ocean water.

Sometimes a person dives and is
For some time poised, suspended like a word
Suspended in inverted commas
Until much later, when someone else stands
And looks towards the decision-laden
Sloshing, slapping, idle water.

The pool is cut into the side
    of a gently
Sloping valley so that any water here,
And there is a considerable prism of it,
Once could not have lingered here.

Sometimes at the far end, the scattered
Semaphore of moving figures
(Boudin's ocean promenade comes to mind,

Pursued by Seurat's river bank
    with much splashing)
Seems to recombine into some semblance
Of a single scene or 'message'.
    Meanwhile,
Splashes appear above the centre
Of this tennis court of water
Where there seems to be no one.

A configuration of serious swimmers
Swimming slow laps
Appears to repeat itself
    but at the same time
Parasolled figures pass outside the fence.

The indolence which wraps events
Like chocolates in their separate foil casings
Affects the storm
    which has perhaps 'decided'
Not to materialise.
    In the water
A person with certain attributes
Puts her arms around
a person with certain attributes.

Fossils laid down under water over a period
Of thousands of years are scarcely slower
Than this upended water and its swimmers:
The pool is clearly
    waiting for someone

To come up with something, a single statement,
A phrase of perhaps no more than line-length,
Which will encompass everything and at last
Lift it bodily over the lapping rim.

Therefore let the hour advance to the siren
    and elated release into lunch
And the typewriter already primed with these phrases.

# Sunburn

Every summer sheds new light
On the whole question of the relation
Between the legs and 'personality'.
Sometimes in shorts that relation

Seems very tenuous indeed
And long legs walking,
Which lead one almost to expect
Antlers, have a character of their own.

The vexed matter of where,
And in what way separately,
Resides the intelligence
Can be confused by sandals with heels

Just as when a person is sunburnt
And the body reveals, through the stencil
Of crossed shoulder straps,
The hours spent reading or dreaming,

That person reveals a readiness
To regard the body as dispensable
Or to some degree separable
From the person who came to the beach.

Thus is born the Platonic disjunction
Which many blame for all the miseries
Of this world. Yet the body
And its outposts of consciousness

Frequently suggest some surrogate
Declamation, a life-history
In the knees, or a three-part biography
In the forearm, or a confession

In the flush of a calf or thigh
Crossed and in time uncrossed
While its 'owner' drinks cordial
At a white plastic table.

And nothing in the vegetable world,
Its leaves leaning towards a window,
Or objects, such as, say, the shoe scraper
Positioned outside old schoolhouses,

For all their mystery, can approach
The puzzling decentralisation,
Geographically speaking, of the body's
Radiation of consciousness.

Perhaps the strange power of the legs
Is evolutionary: bipedal now,
The brain must farm out much consciousness
To prevent falling over.

Tending to discredit determinism
Through variousness and multiplicity,
Strolling limbs, like strolling players,
Breathe and dream and sleep.

Of course, none of the above
Was weighing on him as he sold postcards
In the hour before walking out
And striding towards the nearest machine.

And he is happily determined
To walk with only a lunch pear
To stand upright in evolutionary mode
At the first available typewriter.

## A Brief e e cummings Period

Frank is describing oddities, long shots,
Outriders on the Bell Curve,
To Ken, Larry, Jackson, James,
Clifford, Robert, Jasper,
Including yesterday's strange events
When he detected in Olivetti's,
Strapped to the demonstration machine,
A small nuclear device
Which he perceived at once was activated by the shift key.
This compelled him to avoid
All upper case letters,
Selected symbols and the exclamation point.

# Sailboard

Phenomenological space
Or the phial of clear liquid

In which things happen
'Out there' at the water's edge

In Central Park
Makes him impatient

'To realise on the page'
The sailboard sail falling.

Two sails tilt so as
To form a butterfly.

He is attempting to pin
The butterflies of the actual

To the fluttering baize surface
Of the accommodating lake

And invent or recall
Equations divorced from this world

By their very attempts to condense it,
Inconsequential abstractions

Such as the scientific graffito
$Ba + 2Na = Banana$.

Such a galaxy of approximations
Demands a typewriter, and fast.

# A Vase of Flowers

An indigestible bun eaten on the run
To a rather distant department store
And the typewriters, has resulted in
An uncharacteristically heavy, multifoliate trope:

He has fastened on a subject
Unusually complicated: a garland of flowers,
To express if not the essence of their flowering
Then at least some aspect of the process

By which such clouds, conch shells of cellulose
Unfold, and how all day they consciously
Preside over what happens on the lawns
And in the room. Amenable in the extreme

They invite all conceivable likenesses
And refute none – so that we apply
Quite recklessly and indiscriminately
Haloes of further concentricity

To all their vortices already spilling
Over with the wash of former praise
However imprecise. Already overfilled
They swell with presence, and appear to fill

Something already full, just as a glass
Of water may be carefully overfilled
By adding coin on coin until at last
Its meniscus stands above the rim.

But all this cellular congestion
Proves too much. Indigestion increases.
He lets the flower poem wilt. Instead
He types a Pollock-friendly free-for-all.

## Have a Nice Day

Here I am standing outside Olivetti's. The time
Is about one minute before the mid-point
Of the first day of the rest of your life.

In that minute I am harvesting the universe
And getting ready a sackful to pour over the typewriter.
But it is the way everything is done which matters

Ensuring the highly visible choice of the nicest things
That have happened or turned up recently,
A fruit salad of delectable things we would all like

To see back again but without the husks
And hulls and rinds and piths and pips;
And how important too that the reader should know

That the whole bouquet is offered just for him.
The particulars of its composition matter little
As long as he feels it is the thought which counts.

# Excursions

One day he sets out from the MOMA.
The sun is higher in the sky
Than a cup held to the lips
At an elegant afternoon tea.

He is tagged with a radio transmitter.
His heart rate, his breath, his imaging capacity
Are being closely monitored
On huge screens in the control centre.

On an impulse he enters
A bistro. On the gingham cloth
The light is exceedingly dappled
Like a rabbit motionless

On a moss of shadows.
On a table, a cup and saucer move
Trembling as in Tarkovsky's *Stalker*.
He orders a drink.

Now he is nearing touch-down.
On the typewriter is something resembling
A cup and saucer with coffee and croissants.
It is a strategically placed camera and microphone.

At Houston Control Centre the first pictures
Are coming through. Researchers are jubilant.
There is an air of electric
Expectancy. The computer images are

Looking good. At each revelation
Cheers break out from the crowds
Pressing round the monitors. The room
Is like a dolphin pool at feeding time.

The definition is remarkable. It is becoming clear
That the atmosphere is able to support
Some limited life forms, for example
The simplest thought such as

'Cup', 'saucer', 'white rabbit',
'Ice cold plums', 'artichoke'.
And gravity is obviously such that
Giant leaps are possible and indeed

Pleasantly difficult to resist.
Occasionally he wanders off-camera;
Then, only volcanic craters, what might be sky,
And close-up views of jacket tweed can be seen.

In an unexpected development
When next in camera range, he appears
To be lunching, drinking from a camera.
'I'm not coming back,' he calls out, raising the cup.

'I'll probably go on to Mars and Venus.
I've always wanted to see the former
In post-coital slumber and the latter
Pensive in unsatisfied desire.'

At this, all hell breaks loose at the monitors.
Frantic signal adjustments succeed only
In restoring his receding, inverted image.
'He's gone,' shouts someone. 'We've lost him.'

# Office Hours

Often
He thinks
Of a poetry
Which resembles nothing more
Than a door
On which
Signs
Are displayed
Which are totally
Ambiguous. As an example:
'This office will be open
On Wednesdays only during
The long vacation.'
If only
Somehow
The world
Could be contracted
Into such
Pleasure.

# Today is Another Day

The ring doves' murmur
Echoes the conversation
Of the telephone men
Under the frangipani.

They have come to answer a complaint
That the phone rings,
Even when it would seem
No one is calling.

Something entirely other
Prevents his sleeping.
A light breeze stirs
The blue curtain.

Opening again in the morning,
The yellow day-lily
Feints with the light
And sets out a second typing day.

## At Sunset

Already like a diagram
The waterfall
    Leads the rush towards abstraction.
Standing at the shallow cave
He hears the falls
    Echo from across the valley.
Time and space, not usually
The subject of any
    Meaningful statement, this time burgeon,
And at the roaring sighing cliff
Sharpen his pleasure
    In the ubiquity of the air.
For some things will, it seems, like these
Descending falls
    In seeming thought, seem permanent,
One moment born into the present
Like a breath
    So soon to harden into tracery.

## In Class

To Francis Ponge a poem
Is a lesson from an object.

Asked to take our place
For today's lesson we are slow

To settle down. Someone throws
A book. Another flicks

Pellets soaked in ink.
Patiently our instructor,

A stone shining on the shore
With the froth of seawater

And sand particles a crab
Has left in a bubble,

Waits for us to be ready.
Even after relative order

Is established, we are wayward
And easily distracted

By the splendour about us,
The ocean, diving seabirds,

Clouds piled up
Along the horizon's shipping routes.

We should be taking notes
Or making some sort of summary

But it is difficult here
To maintain our concentration

Particularly as some of us
Are infatuated with our teacher.

But after I place the stone
Carefully in my pocket,

And make my way to Olivetti's,
I feel a renewed desire to learn

And to catch up on any homework
Which the dog has not eaten.

# In the Taxi

Romantically it seemed that all she said
Was accompanied by the fluttering of her eyes
As if she were offering REM sleep
With its most blissful periodic dreams.

She said, *Discuss the decline of the iamb*
*In American poetry as an expression of the rise*
*Of the individual so that experience per se*
*Prevails over metrical and stanzaic form.*

I knew it was a mistake to indulge
In dreams just then and so we bought a flagon
Of golden summer and took off by taxi
To my island retreat. On the way she said,

*Discuss the theory that American poetry*
*Is an attempt to spiritualise the object*
*In the absence of strongly held beliefs in anything else.*
*In your answer make particular reference to*

*Gladiolus spears lining the way*
*And the panorama of found objects.*
I was bemused. I said, 'All
That remains is to find a typewriter.'

From the taxi we saw in that dawn light
A constant panorama of crucial world events,
The unearthly light for instance that accompanied
The end of the dinosaurs, Tulip Mania, the Wall Street Crash.

She said, *Content rather than form*
*Forces the abandonment of all else.*
*We pin our hopes on inventories of objects*
*Colliding with events. Expatiate at length.*

I was delighted. I said, 'Of all
The typewriter repositories in all the world
That you should lead me here. Wait for me.
Keep the meter running. I won't be long.'

# Publication

In those New York days
When everyone was famous
For five minutes,
Celebrities at lunch,
Everyone could write
And everything written was
A 'poem' by which
We mean a gaily
Contented report on conjunctions
Suitable for faxing
Or jotting down on the back
Of a tram ticket bearing
A mystic or intriguing number
(All numbers being intriguing)
Or hummed aloud
In the beguiling underground.
(There's that word *beguiles* again.)
Thus the waiter
In the theme café
Near the typewriter shop
Notes down happily:
'One cappuccino please
And one of those nice
Strawberry cakes
I think they're called
Hummingbird cakes.
They're moist, with
Passion flower, I mean
Passionfruit juice.'
And in taxi cabs while the driver

Composes his own casual cantos
From the crossed legs
And fragments of declamation
Glimpsed in the mirror,
His animated passengers,
Each his own aleatorist,
Record 'Been there' microseconds
After being there, and
'Done that' nanoseconds
After doing whatever it was
They were doing at the time.
One such poem:
'*Glimpsed from a Taxi:*
A Greta Garbo lookalike
Smiles at the concierge
Just as lightning strikes
The window displays
Blacking out a tableau
Of attractive manikins
In which Geometry
Fights off Naturalism
With bunches of dahlias.'
Someone else is looking
At someone else unleashing
A genetic autobiography
In an upturned face.
Someone else again
Is musing with gravity
Over a manhole
Open in the pavement.

Upstairs in a thousand rooms
Psychiatrists are writing poems
Each faithfully based
On the horizontal revelations
Of a thousand automatic writers
Who in turn are inventing
Variations on themes
From 'Mourning Becomes Electra'
And sounding those cadences
In the cool vistas
Of white plaster ceilings
And tasteful floral arrangements
In alabaster bowls.
To all these desktop
Lap-based single-copy
Publishers, these peripatetic
Rhetoricians, the day is
A vase in which to put
The single stem of the specific.
All that remains,
As night falls mysteriously
Like glycerine/water droplets
Down the suspended filaments
Of an enigmatic fountain
In some public foyer,
Is to ensure the safe
And non-polluting disposal
Of all these 'poems'.
Many not written down
Are simply erased by the next;

Others jotted on menus
Or serviettes or wrappers
Can be disposed of
With minimal impact
On the fragile environment.
Always it is to be hoped
That by nightfall these many millions
Of memos to the present
Have found their way
Into various recycling facilities
So that by the following dawn
The next day's anthology
Can begin to be assembled.

# Butterfly Effect Reversed

He walks out into the street
Having just typed a haiku or ten
About the weather
            when
A shower of shimmering rain
A scurry of shimmying currents
Charges down the street.
            A week later
A butterfly a hemisphere away
              trembles.

# More Roads Not Taken

One day standing at the typewriter console
Accelerating through a Toccata and Fugue in D Minor
    With all the stops out
He began a systematic and serious self questioning:
Had he ever, and if not why not,
    Used the word 'ziggurat'
And might it not be possible to express its steps
In terms of quantum leaps? Or consider the plants
    With anthropomorphic names
Like tiger-lilies: might it not be possible
To invent a symbolism entirely composed of them?
    And what other treasures
Had he neglected? Butterflies, fossils, crystals,
Oddities in the physical world such as the fact
    That glass is 'a supercooled liquid'
And not a 'true solid'. The rich resources,
Hitherto overlooked, for motivic invention in such things,
    Even the sadness of things
He had never included in any of these excursions,
Such as the heavenly aspects of vanilla
    Or the flavour of cucumber;
A legion of alternative muses exhibiting themselves,
United only by his inadvertent neglect of them
    Pressed at his frosted memory
Like children's faces pressed at the baker's glass.
He could not include them all. Rather than neglect any,
    He smiled at the salesgirl and left.

Outside in the street everything was even more deafeningly
Trumpeting forth its claim to inclusion in some fragment
    Whether or not he had ever
Noticed or ever given it more than a passing glance.
He felt an incongruous and curious happiness
    At resisting them all.

## Zinnias

One day
He passes
A florist
And then
Typing restlessly
He advances
The page
After every
Second word
As follows.
Keeping themselves
To themselves
The zinnias
Jostle coolly
Each thinking
The other
A conspirator.
Competing reds
And oranges
Harbour plans
For not
Ever moving
From here,
To yield
To none,
Settled firmly
In tiered
Layers overlaid
Each like
An amphitheatre.
Thistle centres

Bristle drily
Putting out
Miniature petals
Curled like
Cats' tongues
Lapping milk.
And even
More importantly
The backs
Of each
Are beach-coloured.
And all
Of this
So far
Says nothing
About that
Inexpressibly rich
Aura filling
The room,
Redon haze,
Sheer presence
Seemingly almost
Independent of
Their presence
And yet
Embracing them,
Floating out
As radically
As they
Soar above
Their leaves.

# Wheelbarrowing

So much also depends
On whether lunch is

Seasonal pears and cheese
Or ham on rye

Or gladiolus spears,
Bright, familiar, wheelbarrow red,

Fraught with pointed comment,
Leaning at every angle

Across the primrose path
To the Olivetti labyrinth.

And on the delay
A hail shower causes

To his stepping out,
As if geological time

Were in competition with
Common or garden varieties.

Then its luminous aftermath,
Its rowan tree glade,

Hail berries melting slowly,
The excess of subject

Implicit in these reds
Charges the waiting typewriter.

# Letter From Fire Island

Since those days when the poem first became
A confessional, orchestrated for sumptuous Mendelssohnian
String octet with much octave doubling and open string bowing,
And Coleridge in his lime tree bower prison
Began to tell it like it is, or was, the idea took root
Of the poem as a kind of decorative obligato or descant
Running above the melodic line of events,
A burbling contained by the instantaneous present.

Before we know it, next thing we know it is
The lateish 20th century and the street has
In many respects replaced the woods. The Chrysler building
With its 'roof' like an Esther Williams bathing cap
Is still beautiful; Ginger Rogers' feather dress is still
Shedding feathers. Everywhere bands of improvisatory
Poets of the immediate criss-cross the city. It is lunch
From about 10 till perhaps 4. They are learning

To pare down their effusions to a simple
Open sandwich on rye or a piece of fruit.
Many are still unable to forego the mayonnaise
Of adjectives. Many get lost by struggling to capture
Rather than simply to accompany or jog with
The endlessly unfolding present. Many of them
Have kept up with the bouncing ball of events
By stringently avoiding repetition, by looking up frequently

And developing a line of very few words.
Thus destinies diverging like taxis are described
And approximations to the whole world set down.
One of the most charming of these ruminant typists
Has mapped out a network of city keyboards.
He will for example drop into one of several shopfront
Cathedrals to tap out in that camphor air
A Cole Porter melody or two, ritzy and rapid.

One day he vanishes. The typewriter salesgirl
Disowns a tear which splashes from her apple lunch
On to her hand as she applies nail polish.
Orson Welles goes on narrating *The War of the Worlds*
And later *The Happy Prince*. In various cinemas
There is scarcely a flicker discernible from the back row.
But on her glass counter a letter appears.
It is addressed 'To John and Ken and others.'

'I was the meat in the sandwich,' it says,
'Between old Sam Taylor saddled with the albatross
Of the Shakespearian, and you lot, streetwise,
Tough and cheerful. From this paradisial palisade
Unexpected yet pleasant enough, here's looking at you.
I'm already enjoying what you're doing and it seems to me
You've got it right. Each word can be a separate
Radiant entity. And don't connect.'

# Solitary Swimmers

    At the sweet ebbing of the season
    Pansies on longer and longer stems

Like summer grass oblivious of the scythe
Still brightly proclaim the profusion principle.

    At the pool, that blue handkerchief
    Dropped on the grass, there are fewer people.

It seems to recede under its ancient trees,
Their shadows dwindling as if with distance,

    And the pansies look a little
    Like the faces of solitary swimmers.

    He has lingered here too long
    And may not type again today.

# Interlude

Frank O'Hara, legend in his own lifetime,
Is selling postcards then curating a MOMA show,
Legendary in its scope and power
With large to very large works by the following:
    Jasper Johns,
    Larry Rivers,
    Joan Mitchell,
    William de Kooning,
    Fairfield Porter
    Norman Bluhm,
    Grace Hartigan,
    Franz Kline,
    Jackson Pollock,
    Robert Motherwell,
All legends in their own lifetimes.

All of the above are standing in the foyer,
All basking in their outstanding eunoia
And radiating alpha and beta rays of fame.

Frank is musing about something legendary
That happened yesterday:

While he was typing at Olivetti's
Cupid touched his forehead – then, even better,
Stroked his hair. Next he seemed to feel
A sensation as of burning oil
Flowing down his arm towards his wrist.
It is as if he has been kissed. Elated,
He types several magical poems
Without afterwards remembering a word.

Today as a consequence he is
Empowered and says — as he often says —

'Since poetry should be between
Two persons and not two pages,
We, all being legends for the ages —
Especially you, Jackson, the perfect model
For everyone who plans to yodel
Through his own discursive poem —

Should leave these bright, curated walls
And step out into the real world

Each casting his glow over the visual field,
Dazzling the citadel.'
    *Remarkably*

*The real world turns out to be legendary.*

Frank, Larry, Joan, Norman, Willem,
Fairfield, Grace, Franz, Jackson and Robert
Step out together and wheel as one,
The sun radiant on their wings
Like geese setting out before winter.

Memorable, seemingly immortal, they cross
The Queensboro Bridge and look down
Over Roosevelt Island.
    Remarkably

The real world turns out to be legendary.

Frank is in fine form looking down
At East River. He says
>'I've said it before –
But I'll say it again. There are only three poets,
Williams, Whitman and poor old Hart,
Who are better than the movies.
>But wait!
Who is that stretched out
In a cloud of light

On the island? Beautiful! Surely –
Can it be James Dean? About whom
I've written four poems, this looming as the fifth?'
Larry says, 'It can't be – and anyway –'
'Yes,' says Frank, 'this creature has *wings*!'

The light is certainly prodigal. Is this
Simply their own reflected glory? Or oriole
Orisons? Or owl feathers shining?
>Or could this glimmer be
Vulcan's gilded carriage parked in a lay-by
Near Queensboro Bridge?
>Fairfield: 'Could this be
The mercurial heels of Mercury?'
>Grace: 'Hey!
I'd almost be prepared to say for sure
It is Juno taking coffee with Ceres.'
>Frank: 'Where?'
'There! Where the river laps against the island.'

       Frank: 'Say!
This is even better than the movies.'

The light increases by several lumens.
The rose clouds resemble flowers.
The sun appears and reappears.

'Now look again at that creature with wings –
And who is that leaning above him?
She's beautiful too. And what is she holding?
A lamp? And has something spilt?'

Murmurs of approval from all ten *flâneurs*.

Legendary status conferred in all directions.

'And look again. Just when you thought
Things couldn't be more exceptional,
There's Venus swimming in the river
Surrounded by her under-age entourage.
*Her petalled feet are on the water.*
(Petalled feet? Who wrote this stuff?)
       But hey!
Look at the sun glancing off the water!'
Larry: 'That's more like a fireball.'

Frank outside MOMA:
'I think – I think that's Apollo.'

# Cupid and Psyche

Ballet after Apuleius

In a certain city, a certain king and queen
Had three daughters, all most beautiful
But one surpassingly.
                      Readers will
At once remember Cinderella
                and Beauty
In Perrault's tales –
                    Cinderella who
Engages with a pumpkin meaningfully
And Beauty who will save her father – and
Transform the Beast.
                    They will recall also
The ambiguous slippers made of glass or fur –
And other even more resplendent cases
Of three sisters, two malevolent.

This surpassing beauty's name was Psyche.

Admirers came from distant lands by sea
To view this marvel of the universe,
To describe whom, one is soon obliged to allow
Everything may seem like something else:
                Her beauty
Like a grove of almond trees in flower
Or like a mirror held towards the sky –
Beauty which to detail
Must break these strong iambic bands:

    Psyche was like the women painted
            by Peter Lely;

She was like the self-portrait
Of Elizabeth Vigée Lebrun in her hat
Or more generally
Like the entrancing blankness
Of the blue planet's face
Seen from outer space –
Or like Emma Thompson flying near the ceiling
In *Angels in America*.

Venus as a consequence is irate.
As a winner of beauty contests everywhere
She feels neglected and incensed. She frowns
And, quite remarkably, looks past her pique.
'I'm supposed to be the apple of the eye –
The ant's pants, the radiance, enigmatic
Ship launch, divine –
                   And yet this ordinary girl
Is getting all the social media time.
My altars are deserted, candles once
In rows of votive praise have guttered out.
But I'll erase this wide-eyed *tabula rasa*.'

So saying, Venus found her son Cupid sleeping
After firing off a few too many arrows.
'Darling son,' she said, 'you see that girl –
Yes there – that flashy one who looks quite cheap –
                   The one who is lazing about
In front of all those sycophantic fans?
Avenge me – that is all I ask. You can.
Make her fall for some old derelict.'
At which she kissed her son immodestly.

Next,
Venus is flying, free of iambics,
Then her petalled feet are on the water.
Everything is almost unpleasantly calm.
Daughters of Nereus sing
Like the Vienna Boys' Choir –
Very sweetly, perhaps over-sweetly.
Tritons cavort obligingly.
Others hold a mirror. Yet others
Shade her from the sun.
Readers might even, for a moment,
See Gloria Swanson in *Sunset Boulevard*.

Then she water-skis for the cameras
Holding a rosebud rope,
Followed by synchronised swimming
Like a prequel to 'By A Waterfall'
With Ruby Keeler in *Footlight Parade*.

Meanwhile – the real world being multiple –
An odd thing happens. Unexpectedly,
Against all reason, Psyche languishes;
While much *admired* she is never courted, since
Perfection places one beyond the pale
And other-worldliness provokes unease.

> Her father consults the Oracle.
> Everything seems highly irregular –
> Verse-wise and sage-wise.
> Apollo, speaking through the Sybil, recommends
> The rarely proposed *funeral wedlock*.

    Psyche must be exposed on a high rock
    To await some unpleasantness, some demon lover –
    Like Giulietta Massina hung out to dry,
    Put upon in all of her husband's films.

Arrayed in bridal veil fair Psyche pales.
The shops are closed. The crowded city mourns.
Pallid torches burn with black ash.
Music modulates to Lydian mode.
Her father and her mother are distraught.
Processions follow them towards the cliffs,
With so much turbulence in Nature caused
By beauty concentrated so unnaturally.

    Led to the high rock she must wait
    Without rhyme or reason or metre
    An unknown bridegroom – perhaps,
    According to the Oracle, a monster.
    She is alone, betrayed by her beauty,
    The world seemingly against her
    Like Joan Crawford walking into the sea.

    Meanwhile Venus has returned
    From her elated cavorting
    To look at her reflection with trepidation
    Reminding the reader perhaps
    Of the Wicked Queen in *Snow White*:
        Mirror, Mirror on the wall –

> The mirror into which Venus stares
> Held by two Tritons in a flattering light
> Says, 'You're certainly not at your best
> But the exposure of Psyche
> May help you pass the test.'

Psyche meanwhile is trembling on the rock
Expecting some dark power to force her back
And give some meaning to the mysterious terms
Of *Nuptial Pyre* or *Funeral Bride*.

> Suddenly with a rustling
> Such as the reader might sense
> In *Spelt From Sybil's Leaves*
> Where Hopkins' syllables
> Sound like ancient pebbles in water,
> Zephyr arrives without disturbing,
> In the least, cicada and birdsong
> And lifts her up gently
> And on his breath carries her down
> Enswathed loosely in her dress
> Onto the folds of a field.

The reader will recall Charles Perrault
In what comes next.
                She falls into a sleep –
That holding pattern devoutly to be wished –

And then on waking finds herself amazed
And startled at the pleasure house of gods,
A golden palace and a palisade
Impossible to describe.

But here at least are several furnishings:
                 Walls embossed in silver,
With leopards and various wild and tender beasts
Nuzzling and parading, almost real;
The floor inlaid with patines (yes!) of gold
With more gold everywhere which radiantly
Creates its own light without the sun.

    The reader may remember
    Images of the lost Russian Amber Room
    And, removing the amber,
    Substitute on every wall
    Holograms and voices and music.

A banquet silently appeared – with wine –
And many courses endlessly renewed.
A disembodied voice ensured her calm.

    And more discursively
    She wandered from room to room
    With unseen music. Dusk fell.
    The private sun glowed still.

>Psyche in bed in silver light
>Hearing a sound holds
>Luminous fears. She trembles.
>Now there enters
>Her unknown husband. All
>That has been without seems enclosed.
>She sees only his weight and shadow.
>Dawn finds her alone.

Every night her husband enters her bed
Only to leave at dawn. Delight becomes
Infected with her curiosity.
The present cannot cast aside the past
And shadows gather round her empty days.

>He says, 'Your sisters are
>A real and present danger.
>You must not see my face.
>But surely that is a small price
>For the splendours of our nights.
>Yet your sisters will pursue you
>And make demands you must resist.'

Dawn made fresh shadows on the walls. He said,
'Do not let their vain duplicity
Deceive you into fruitless questioning
About our destiny, or urge you still
To seek to see my face. For they will try.'

And Psyche said, 'Dear husband, I would not
Put any of this happiness at risk.'

She held him in her arms 'long and small'
Recalling Wyatt's 'newfangleness'.
She revelled in the nights.
She said, 'I love you to distraction;
Even Cupid himself could not compare.'

One day she says,
'But, dearest, grant me this one wish. Let Zephyr
Bring my sisters here as he brought me.'

Her husband, leaving her arms, agrees.

The sisters shriek so loudly on the rock
That Psyche hears them and summons Zephyr.
The sisters seeing the treasures in the house
At once ply her with questions. 'Psyche, dear,
Who is the master of this luxury?
When will you tell us who he is?'

Psyche is wary and says merely,
'He is a young man
Who spends the days hunting in the mountains.'
She gives them precious gifts.

The sisters, travelling back on Zephyr's wings
At once are fuming and consumed with envy.
'*Our* husbands cannot rise to this.'
'*Our* husbands give us nothing. Mine is bald.'
'And mine has rheumatism and demands
I spend my days as nursemaid to his whims.'

Envy hatches plots
As large as dodo eggs;
One sister says,
        'Our glass
Is half empty.'
The other says,
        'Speak for yourself.
Mine is shattered on the floor.
Our sister has hundreds of glasses
All of them overflowing.'

    Returning home, they hide
    Their gifts of gold plate and jewels.

Again her husband whispered in Psyche's ear
As she entwined her arms around him. 'Listen.
And beware your sisters' guile. They will attempt
To make you wish to see my face. And so
You must be strong and fend off great calamity.
Your murderous sisters would destroy us both.
Ignore them if you can – because you have
A greater task, to nourish in your womb
One who may – unless you confide in them –
Be radiant and divine, not merely mortal.'

    Psyche revelled in this revelation
    And promised to be vigilant.

But then she said, 'Let Zephyr, one last time,
Bring my sisters here to visit me
And I will be most vigilant.'

> But she was, alas,
> Like Little Red Riding Hood
> Setting out to meet the Wolf,
>
> Or like Arletty as Garance
> In *Les Enfants du Paradis*
> Lost in the seething crowd.

She wakes soon after dawn. The indoor sun
Is equalled by the menacing orb outside.
The sisters leap from Zephyr's airy car
Intent on solving mysteries.

Despite her protestations in the dark,
'I am content to see your face at last
In our son's face – and I will take great care
In everything my sisters might devise –'
Poor Psyche soon relinquishes all she has.

> The sisters flatter and cajole.
> 'So you are to be a mother.
> Wonderful. But who, we wonder,
> Can the father be? We worry
> Dearest sister, about you.'

A second line of attack:
'Remember the Pythian Oracle
That you were to be exposed on the rock
And wed to a wild beast –
Who knows if this may have happened?
We are only doing our duty
Out of our concern for you.'

Poor Psyche indeed!
The simple-minded girl
Quite forgets her promise
As her sisters advance this argument.
'This is our advice:

You must at night secure a knife and lamp,
Well charged with oil, and when the serpent sleeps,
Go barefoot, silent, raise the knife,
Unshield the lamp and in its righteous blaze
Gaze on, then strike your demon captor's head.'

The reader might be reminded
Of Bette Davis in *The Little Foxes*
Or deviousness in a thousand plays.

The sisters left. Reluctant Zephyr shook
His head, but in so doing wafted them
In placid currents far from Psyche's room,
Where, tossed on breaking waves of fear and doubt,
And buffeted by endless turbulence,
She washes in the swell between the waves.

    That night her husband returns.
    Every irregularity must follow,
    Both metrical and moral.
    He prospers on the fields of love,
    He falls into sleep. She rises.
    She uncovers the lamp.

And what she saw was doubtlessly a god
Radiant in sleep. She gazed still.
She tried to hide the knife. She gazed still.
She saw a milk-white neck and golden hair
Which shone with such great brilliance that the lamp
Seemed suddenly uncertain. And there were wings!
This god had dew-white wings with golden webs.
His body shines like marble from Carrera
And, amazingly, beside him lies a quiver
Spilling arrows. This is Cupid! This
Is the god whose child moves in her womb!

    She gazes still, transfixed
    As if she gazes at a photograph
    Emerging in its fixative.

She takes an arrow tentatively from the quiver,
She accidentally pricks her thumb. Blood flows.
She has by chance been made to love Love.

But now another accident occurs.
The lamp held high above the god has spilled
A drop of burning oil. Cupid is hurt.
His shoulder burns with dark remorseful fire
So that he wakes, surrounded by betrayal
And flies away at once into the clouds.

    Catastrophe turns to crisis.
    Psyche clings to the god's right leg
    But falls.
               Cupid from a cypress
    Speaks to her:
               'Foolish girl,
    I disobeyed my mother Venus
    Who ordered you to be bound
    In a degrading love.
            Instead
    I took one arrow to myself
    So as to love you.

    I warned you of great danger
    But now everything is broken.

I took my fiercest arrow from its quiver
And struck myself so as to fall into love
With you, with you, with you.'

            He vanishes.

Now Psyche is desolate.
She is on the banks of a stream,
As desolate as a certain Princess
Filmed alone in front of the Taj Mahal.

Psyche watched her husband fly away,
She watched his wings merge faintly into clouds
Then threw herself into the nearby stream.

A darkening shadow spread across the river.
The sun moved to a distant quarry face.

> But the river out of respect
> Bore her onto the bank.
> Here by chance lay Pan
> With Echo in his arms
> Learning the art of repetition.

The goat-god smiled. 'I see in your tottering steps,
Your tears, your pallid face, you are in love.
I may be a mere rustic but I know
Unnatural death can never help your cause.
Rather,
      intensify your praise of Cupid
Who is the greatest of the gods –
Whose arrows can affect us all – and hope
At last to earn again his blissful favours.'

    Emboldened by the herdsman-god she left
And wandered hopefully.
                By chance (again)
She reached one sister's house. She said, 'Remember –

    Dear sister – your advice
    Which I followed.
             It all turned out
    Very strangely.' She described
    Her startlement at unshielding the lamp,
    Then her husband's beauty
    And the fateful drop of oil.

'My husband said, "For this foul crime I must
Insist you leave this bed at once. Instead,"
(I found this strange) "I will wed your sister."'

And hearing this, that calculating sister,
Overcome by lust and jealousy,
That Cupid was himself the secret husband –
Resolved to leave her home. Calling Zephyr
She leaped from the appointed rock.
              This time,
No intervention saved her fatal fall
And birds of prey and wild beasts benefited.

    Psyche travelled on
    Reaching the second duplicitous sister.
         'Remember,
    Dear sister – your advice, which I followed…'

And she related the same strange story
– Lamp, wings, arrows –
And repeated the remarkable claim
That Cupid now resolved to marry her sister.

And the second sister
Hastened to the rock, summoned Zephyr
And fell, through calm breezeless air,
From crag to crag,
To her ignominious death.

Psyche remained Love's captive.
In his mother's rooms
Her husband groaned
Still languishing from the burn.

     Venus, meanwhile,
Neglecting her responsibilities,
Was diving, surfacing and splashing,
Swimming in the bright cerulean sea.

People were murmuring:
Venus was neglectful,
Her son was indulging himself
With some secret love. Venus
Was spending the days bathing.
     At last
A white tern flew out to sea
To tell her of her son's fever
And of the rumours:
         'Gaps in Nature

Are widening. The palace of the gods
Is empty and unguarded.
You, Venus, former Immaculate
Are lazing about on beaches
Or floating with nereids between waves…
People feel the time
Is out of joint.'

Venus discovers Cupid has,
Of all people, taken up with Psyche
Who she had instructed
Should be burdened with someone disreputable.
Reluctantly Venus dries herself
Leaving her nymphs in the foam
And returns to find
– Yes, as the bird had said –
Her wayward son unwell in bed.

Even so she is furious
And shouts unreasonably, 'You lecher!
Taking up with that girl!'

She shouted loudly and fiercely
Like Anna Magnani
In *Rome Open City*.

She rebuked her son
For betraying her with Psyche
As Maria Casares as Baptiste's wife
In *Les Enfants du Paradis*
Rebukes him for pursuing Garance
Who is a convenient absence.

She resolves to blunt his arrows, break his bow,
Put out his torch and then insist
He shave his golden locks which she – his own
Misguided mother – gilded with her hands.

    Meanwhile in the anonymous world
    Here and there and elsewhere
    Psyche is still lost.

    And Psyche is troubled.
    The present tense irregularly
    Alternates with the past.

Venus rushes out into the world
Enraged and unforgiving. There she meets
Juno and Ceres who observe:
            'We cannot help but note
Your beauty is diminished by this rage.'

    Of course they knew already
    With god-vision everything
    Fulminating Venus described.

    They said,
        'Be fair.
    You forget your son
    Who looks angelically young
    Is of an age to fall
    For someone looking like polished marble.'

But Venus, unassuaged
And lacking all resourcefulness
Demanded to be carried back
Towards the mellifluous sea –
Where the comforting Waves cried
In unison and singly:

'You, who were mysteriously born from us,
Are still beautiful despite sorrows,
Particularly when you water-ski
On an open shell
Or perform formation diving sequences
With your water nymphs, or when
You surface face first
So that your hair streams behind you.'
After this Venus was partially assuaged,

While Psyche, tearful, wandered in the past
Which kept repeatedly, like some neap tide,
Returning to engulf the present.

She wandered without knowing where she went.

She found a temple with a granary
Within which sickles lay amongst the corn
In great confusion.
                Almost without thought
In her distraction she arranged the grain
In garlands, tidying the implements
And putting everything in order.

    Ceres entered,
    And praised her diligence
    But explained that she could not offer help
    Because of her kinship with Venus,
    Who was, she said,
    Looking uncharacteristically distraught
    And not herself and therefore
    Not quite at her best.

Rebuffed and disappointed,
          Psyche walked
Again through forests under mist and cloud
While thunder like a distant afterthought
Came distantly behind its lightning.
          Next
Another temple set about with signs
Proclaiming 'Juno' 'Juno' 'Juno' 'Juno'
On every side…

    Psyche brushed away her tears
    And prayed aloud,
    'Sister and consort of great Jove
    You who are worshipped in Samos
    In the shrine which witnessed your birth,
    You who are seen in Carthage,
    Worshipped there as a virgin
    Riding the clouds on a lion,
    And revered in the citadel of Argos,
    You who are called Zygia

And, in the west, Lucina,
You Juno, Juno proclaimed here,
Revered as protector of pregnant women,
Save me from multiple perils.'

But Juno appearing after an interval
Said, 'Believe me,
I would like to help but unfortunately
I am bound by loyalty
To my daughter-in-law Venus
Who of late has looked
In need of a little more mascara.'

Psyche, alone in the firmament
And yet beset on every side
By self-absorbed, self-serving gods,
Concludes:
    'My last remaining path
Out of this gilded labyrinth
Must be to summon a man's courage
And confront my mother-in-law.'

But, just now, Venus
Has wearied of splashing about
And surfing on shells
And fending off compliments.

And failing to confront her son's mistress,
She flies into the heavens on the car
Of sculpted gold which Vulcan made for her
On her betrothal day.
                    Four fleece-white doves
Submitted to the yoke then lifted off
Into the breezes of the stratosphere
With sparrows chattering to complement
The honeyed harmonies of other birds.

    She confronted Jupiter
    Demanding the services of Mercury.
    Mercury was obliging.

    'This,' said Venus, handing him a paper,
    'Is the name of the low-life piece of fluff
    Who has entrapped my poor demented son.
    Find her.'

    And Mercury showing
    An impressive set of heels
    Says, 'Never fear, your Gorgeousness.
    I'll take her a severe message,
    Payment on delivery.'

So Mercury then trumpeted abroad
The proclamation:
                    'If any man can find
A king's delinquent daughter, Psyche by name,
Let him report to Mercury
And as reward he shall receive
From Venus herself several startling kisses.'

Venus is at home again
With Vulcan's wrought-gold carriage parked outside.

When Psyche sees decrees on every side
Demanding her discovery, she is
Still more emboldened.

Destiny appears to lead her on
To face the music with her mother-in-law,
A music promising to be
Discordant in the extreme
(Like the music of Xenakis still to come
From this same place in several millennia).

    She reaches the door.
    She is seized by the hair.
    Several of Venus' handmaids
    And hangers-on, Habit, Care, Sorrow,
    Abuse her, tearing her clothes.

Venus joined their railing cries with zest
'To think that I will be obliged to be
A grandmother in my youthful prime!
              And worse,
The boy will be a bastard, since the banns
Were never properly approved.

You have a nerve,' shrieked Venus, 'coming here
While my poor boy is at death's door with burns
Which you inflicted. Reckless, shameless girl!'

Then Venus thought of Hercules
And mused,
              'I'll set this upstart several tasks.'

    The first was to sort a huge confusion
    Of wheat and barley and millet
    And poppy seeds and lentils
    And chickpeas into separate heaps.

    And leaving Psyche
    Like Cinderella amongst the ashes,
    Venus, looking a thousand serstices,
    Set out for a wedding banquet.

But Venus did not take into account
The Kingdom of the Insects.
              Ants arrived –
It seemed spontaneously like bees
In Virgil – and marching against injustice,
With military precision completed the task.

    Venus arrived home
    Flushed with wine and perfume,
    Garlanded with roses,
    Wearing the beauty of dissipation
    And saw the task done.

Annoyed by this unexpected order
She devised another impossibility.

'*Woolgathering*! That is tomorrow's task.
You see that river winding past its bank
Where wandering sacred sheep occasionally
Are brushed by trees? Occasionally
A precious tuft is caught. Tomorrow's task
Is gathering – by hook or by crook – these shreds
Which then come back to me. There'll be no time
For you to stand and stare. *No woolgathering.*'

    And Venus, even more fiercely,
    Said, 'Of course you may not
    See my son. He is sick with burns.
    Here is a crust of bread. Now sleep.'

Next morning Psyche contemplates the task.
A reed which had for many years
Been ruminating at the river's edge
Said, 'Let me sound a note of caution here;
Those sheep are very savage in noon heat;
But wait till dusk and they will not attack.
So take your time.
Make a simple pan pipe from some reeds
And while away the day with melody,
Then shake the branches in the cool of day
And carry back a cloud of golden fleece.'

Returning with a cloud of golden fleece,
Poor Psyche finds that all is of no avail.
For unrelenting Venus now invents
Tomorrow's even more preposterous task
Involving cliffs and peaks and dangerous ravines.

'You see where at the crag
The ravine feeds a black spring
Which feeds the Styx marshes?
Take this jar and there
From the very summit
Between two cliffs
Bring me its ice-cold water.'

When Psyche reached the mountain it was clear
The last ascent was quite impossible.
The water cried out from its waterfall –
*Beware. Do not proceed. Do not expect*
*Water to provide solution.*
            Then suddenly

Jove's wide-winged eagle swooped down through the spray
And, recognising Cupid's wife, exclaimed,
'Do you, poor creature, think that you alone
Could seize the waterfall (et cetera et cetera)
The dangers are extreme (et cetera et cetera)
The waters of the Styx are feared by gods
So how might you (et cetera et cetera)
What's more (et cetera et cetera)'
(Then followed further cautionary interludes
Which Psyche did not fully understand)
Until at last –
'Give me the urn!'

The eagle gave a kind of godly shriek
Then seized the gilded vessel in its beak
And, with strong wingbeats reached the very peak.

Psyche marvelled at the sound
Which drowned out the waterfall.

She watched the eagle like a hummingbird
Fluttering briefly at the icy crest
And then returning.

She took the brimming urn.
Venus seemed again displeased
Yet strangely conciliatory.
         She said
'This is the genuine article.
You are clearly capable
But there is one last thing:'

Venus sighed heavily
'It's been several years
Since Paris gave me the prize
And I gave him Helen
And incurred collateral damage
I don't like to think about
– The war to begin all wars.
And in that time I may have lost
A little of my former freshness
And perhaps even some of that glow…

So this is what I'm asking you to do:
Take this special casket. Keep it sealed.
Descend into that ghostly Underworld
And there find Proserpine. Say to her,

"Venus asks that you might send a little
Of your beauty – just enough perhaps
To last a day." Tell her I've used a lot
In caring for an ailing son. Just say
I need it for the Theatre of the Gods.'

> Psyche thought but said nothing. Yes,
> Her beauty at its apogee
> Now had elements of apology,
> Her beauty once unsurpassed
> Seemed to be rushing towards the past.

This was the most dangerous task of all.
She feared descending into Tartarus,

> Yet she thought:
> 'Lucretius urges
> That the Underworld is only an emblem
> Of all that's worst here –
> And I have surely seen all that.'

> But such elusive cheerfulness faded
> And soon she found she was considering
> The fastest way to get to Tartarus
> Would be to leap from the crag
> And take the express route
> And sever soul from body. She climbed a tower.

> She was teetering
> Without order or repose
> Uncertain which path to choose.
> But suddenly the tower spoke:

'Poor child, do not leap.
In this part of the world
We know about souls.
Without yours you may well
Sink to Tartarus
But never be able to return.'

Then followed a rigmarole of instructions
Involving nearby Sparta, barley cakes
Soaked in wine and honey,
A lame donkey loaded with wood,
Its lame driver whose pleas must be ignored,
Charon and his ferry, two coins
To be held in the mouth,
Several ancient female weavers
Whose cries must also be resisted.

'Now are you listening? *Please* remember this.
You must have two coins in your mouth.
You must carry two barley cakes –
Charon needs a coin for each crossing;
A savage dog will need to be held off
With barley cake. And this will happen twice.
And then you will discover Proserpine;
But do not join her in her rich repast,
Ask for bread and sit down on the ground,
And when returning do not – I repeat – do not
Unseal the casket you are carrying.'

All this she performed dutifully:
Coins, barley cakes, donkeyman ignored,
Ancient weavers rebuffed,
Styx crossed, dog placated, Proserpine met,
Banquet declined, the crust of bread, casket
Taken, filled and returned. The second coin,
The second dog placated. And so on and so on.

In fact every stricture was observed
Until the last:
*Do not peer into the casket.*

Then Psyche, much relieved to see the light
Began to reason thus:
    'There's no one here.
Only the forest with its fringe of sun,
Only the harmless stream and encouraging birds
Who seem to say, *Rules may be broken here.*
*Everyone should be allowed to fly.*

So here I am – still hoping that one day
I might see my husband once again
And he see me. In which case would it not
Be sensible to ensure I'm at my best?'

 She was convinced.
 She unsealed the casket,
 Disaster once again strode abroad.

As coloured amphorae mellifluous
In opalescent water shimmering
Raised to the surface fade and seem like lead,
So beauty on exposure to the air
Became at once transformed to Stygian sleep.

> So once again
> Psyche courted malevolent Fortune.
>
> She was covered and clouded in oblivion.
> Stygian darkness closed round her
>
> And she collapsed holding the casket.

But Cupid's wound had healed. Thinking only
Of Psyche, he escaped his prison room
By flying through a window. Psyche lay
Insensible but beautiful. At once
He scooped up Stygian sleep like caramel
Returning it to the casket.
               Psyche stirred.
The lightest touch of Cupid's finest arrow
Restored to her a startled ardency.

He said,
'You are beautiful again – but far too curious.'

He said, 'And now
You must at once
Hasten to complete my mother's task.
The rest I will facilitate.'
At which he soared into clouds.
She went at once to Venus with the casket.

Above the cloud line Cupid visited Jupiter
As suppliant, intent on seeking help.
'Well, I don't know,' said Jupiter. 'Of course,
We gods – as you well know – have too much power
And tend to get in one another's way.
And even you, dear boy, have been somewhat
Over-enthusiastic with the bow;
How many times I've taken in the breast
Your arrows, making me ridiculous,
To hare off suddenly in strange disguise
Pursuing anyone and everyone
And putting Nature's Laws at risk on earth.

But I don't mind. It can be dull up here
And I can overlook your boyish ways.
How can I help? What would you like –
A slap-up feast? A wedding? Royal games?
Perhaps confer an immortality?
But, in return, should there appear on earth
A girl of some pre-eminent loveliness
(Of course not Psyche – she is yours)
I'd hope you'd intervene on my behalf.'

All this was affably arranged.
Mercury was summoned and set out
To gather every god and demi-god –
On pain of hefty fines – to save the date.
For Jupiter ascending to his hyper-throne
Spoke through his powerful megaphone:

'New and old conscripted deities
As listed in the Register of Muses,
You obviously all know this young man well.
I have decided his hot-bloodedness,
Which has, you will agree, affected us all,
Should now be curbed at last by mystical bonds.
Domestic maintenance should fill his days
And see less arrows darkening the air.'

And now he turns to Venus. 'Daughter dear,
You are – I must say – looking beautiful;
Proserpine makes her unguents well.
But still you look distraught. Don't be concerned
Your son is marrying beneath his class.
I'll fix all that. Just watch me now.'

He summoned Psyche. Pomp and Circumstance
Accompanied this public ceremony.
He handed her a cup of pure ambrosia
And said, 'Take this. Take immortality.'

> Psyche took the cup.
> Everything seemed beautiful
> As beautiful as Edwige Feuillère's voice
> Or Catherine Deneuve's gaze in *The Last Metro*.

A wedding feast ensued. Rare nectars flowed.
Vulcan cooked up a storm. Apollo sang.
The Muses danced. The Graces sprinkled scent,
While Venus looked extremely beautiful.
The Seasons scattered flowers. In Cupid's arms
Psyche felt at last impending calm.

Thus was Psyche wed at last to Cupid
And, when her time arrived, gave birth to one,
A daughter whom we call Pleasure or Happiness.

Lightning Source UK Ltd.
Milton Keynes UK
UKHW020713090820
367908UK00011B/645